G000065953

COMPANION TO THE FEASTS OF MARY

by
J.B. Midgley

*All booklets are published thanks to the
generous support of the members of the
Catholic Truth Society*

CATHOLIC TRUTH SOCIETY
PUBLISHERS TO THE HOLY SEE

CONTENTS

INTRODUCTION

Mary's Place in the Christian's Journey

The Second Vatican Council (1962-65) in the eighth chapter of *'Lumen Gentium'* - the *'Dogmatic Constitution on the Catholic Church'* (1965), enshrines Marian theology and devotion in the truths of faith and their articulation. After her Divine Son, and never equated with Him, Our Lady is esteemed before all as a unique member of the Church in her faith and charity and as its most honoured model. It is of great comfort that she remains united to all of us, her family, who look for salvation. Though Mother of the Son of God made man, she is, like us, of 'Adam's stock'.

To have recourse to her cannot lessen or enlarge the infinite dignity and efficacy of Christ, the Sole Mediator. Of course, no created being can compare with the Incarnate Word and Redeemer but Our Lord shares His Priesthood with His people among and through whom His loving kindness is made manifest. In the same way, as in the case of Mary, the unique mediation of the Redeemer stimulates, rather than excludes, a participation and co-operation which is varied but which originates from the One Source. *(cf 62 LG)*

Her elevation, by dogma and tradition, emanates from authentic Christology and is directed to faith in Christ as true God and true man. In her, scripture and tradition, the old and new people of God and the mysteries of faith come together and are presented anew. Devotion to her widens the human dimension of faith wherein the reasoning of the intellect keeps company with the warmth of the heart. *(cf 65 LG)*

In 1964, Pope Paul VI, on the feast of the Presentation of the Most Blessed Virgin *(November 21st)*, conferred on her the title *'Mother of the Church'*, so reminding us that she is the Mother of all Christians through her motherhood of the world's Saviour. Four years later, he reiterated the Council's teaching in a series of weekly talks on Our Lady as one embraced within the Divine Trinitarian relationship which we adore. "As we cannot form an idea of Christ without reference to the truths of the Gospel regarding His Incarnation and the Redemption, so we cannot ignore the presence of Mary in every mystery of Christ's salvific mission." *(cf 61 LG)*

Paul VI and devotion to Mary

In 1974, Pope Paul delivered his felicitous Apostolic Exhortation *'Marialis Cultus'* for the "right ordering and development of devotion to the Blessed Virgin Mary in the context of the theological, liturgical and spiritual renewal intended by the Council. Appropriately, he chose the feast of the Presentation of the Lord *(February 2nd)*, recalling our gratitude to His Mother, for its publication. The following lines attempt a respectful and relevant synthesis.

Devotion to the Blessed Virgin originates in Christ, the source and centre of the ecclesial community, in Whom it finds its complete expression and efficacy. It reflects the Church's piety, the singular part played by Mary in obedience to the intentions of the Father's plan of Redemption and the unity of her Son's Mystical Body into which all are newly born through the assent of the second Eve. The maternal love shown by Mary and the Church inspires our reciprocation. When we celebrate and live with the Divine Mysteries in faith, charity and union with Christ, when we call upon Him and, in the Holy Spirit, worship the Father, our spiritual attitude has been nurtured by Mary's example.

Such devotion is permeated by the themes of the Gospel message which sustain the Church's Apostolic mission. The Liturgy, rich in doctrine, exercises a pastoral care as it reveals again the work of salvation through the annual arrangement of its feasts. The Holy Father points to the devotion's ecumenical character and its search for that social justice expected in Mary's 'Magnificat'. Her veneration as *'Theotokos'*, God-bearer and Help of Christians, unites Catholic and Orthodox Churches with Anglicans in appreciating her position in the Christian life and with the Churches of the Reform in their love of the Sacred Scriptures wherein God is praised by her rejoicing spirit. The power of the Most High which overshadowed the Virgin of Nazareth urges our acclaim of the Handmaid to whom the Almighty has done great things. The same Holy Spirit gathers, rather than divides, all who believe in her Son and will guide us away from a misleading and inhibiting exaggeration to a doctrine unclouded and supportive of unity.

A woman for our times, Mary mirrors the expectations of all women who seek their entitled participation in decision-making. In her dialogue with God they can recognise a responsible consent to co-operation in the Incarnation, an event of matchless importance. Her choice of virginity is no rejection of the values of the married state but a courageous decision to dedicate herself to God. She was no timid submissive of repellent piety but a woman of conviction who proclaimed loudly that God vindicates the humble and strips the powerful of privilege. She knew poverty, suffering, flight and exile, undertook a fraught journey to help an elderly cousin, adopted her universal children as she watched her Son die in agony and fortified the faith of the early apostolic community. The model disciple of the Lord, Mary helps establish an earthly realm while journeying to one which is heavenly and everlasting. She works for justice, the liberation of the oppressed and the solace of the needy; she is the active witness of the love which enthrones Christ in human hearts and, having walked with us in this vale of tears, has prepared our share in her eternal joy.

Pope John Paul II

The papacy and pastoral teaching of Pope John Paul II, have been characterised by his personal devotion to Our Lady and his desire to share with us the significance of Marian theology. In his encyclical *'Redemptoris Mater'*, written to herald the Marian Year 1987-8, he urged a renewal of Marian spirituality and following his predecessor, spoke of Mary as a woman of the people who exercises a tender care for the poor, who in her virginity and motherhood illuminates God's creation of femininity and the noble destiny of Woman. He refers to her 'Magnificat' in like manner where she announces the liberation bestowed by God who puts the mighty down from their thrones, raises the lowly, feeds the hungry and sends the rich away empty. *(cf Luke 1:45-55)* She is a model of action, courage, initiative and perception. She gives birth to her Baby while homeless, escapes a murderous ruler, takes refuge in a foreign country, remains at the foot of the Cross on which her Son is unjustly executed and is there at the birth of His Church. The new Eve accompanies the new Adam, from the Annunciation, through His birth, the marriage at Cana, His passion and Death and the coming of the Holy Spirit at Pentecost.

It has been the Pope's practice to conclude his communications to the Church with a dedication to Mary.

A recent example is in *'Towards the Third Millennium'* (1994) where he entrusts the Church's whole period of preparation to "the unassuming young woman of Nazareth who, two thousand years ago, offered to the world the Incarnate Word". As in *'Veritatis Splendor'* (1993), his encyclicals conclude with a typical prayer:

"O Mother of Mercy, watch over all people that the Cross of Christ may not be emptied of its power, that man may not stray from the path of good or become blind to sin but may put his hope ever more fully in God Who is rich in mercy. *(Eph 2:4)* May he carry out the good works prepared by God beforehand *(cf Eph 2:10)* and so live completely for the praise of His glory. *(Eph 1:12)*"

The ancient Roman Canon (Eucharistic Prayer 1) commemorates the Mother of the Lord in terms of doctrine and devotional inspiration: "In union with the whole Church we honour Mary, the ever-Virgin Mother of Jesus Christ our Lord and God." Similarly, Eucharistic Prayer 3 expresses our desire to share with Mary the eternal destiny God wishes for us: "'May He make us an everlasting gift to You (Father) and enable us to share in the inheritance of Your Saints with Mary, the Virgin Mother of God." From the rising of the sun to its going down, the daily commemoration at the heart of the Divine Sacrifice is offered as the most expressive form of veneration the Church can pay to the Blessed of the Most High. *(cf Luke 1:28; 'Marialis Cultus', 10)*

The following pages were first collected to help a personal preparation for the feasts of Our Lady and rely almost wholly upon Sacred Scripture, the Fathers of the Church and the Liturgy. Generally, selections are allowed to speak their own message but where the collector's observations intrude the decline must be forgiven. Some years ago, these were shared with fellow parishioners in Liturgy Groups and in contributions to the Rite of Christian Initiation of Adults. There was a kind suggestion that a wider audience might find useful the lines of thought prompted by an anthology from sources not always readily available.

To the Feasts of Our Lady is added a consideration of the Holy Family. This seemed appropriate for it was through the Family at Nazareth - Joseph and Mary - that the Son of God entered human history two thousand years ago. Of Saint Joseph perhaps it is enough to quote St Teresa: "I cannot comprehend how we can contemplate the Queen of Angels giving, night and day, her maternal cares to the Child Jesus without rendering thanks, at the same time, to her chaste spouse for the assistance he so generously gave to the Mother and Son,"

Downham Market, October 1998.

SOLEMNITY OF MARY, MOTHER OF GOD

January 1st

Origins and Significance

"In the revised ordering of the Christmas period it seems to us that the attention of all should be directed towards the restored Solemnity of Mary, the holy Mother of God. This celebration, placed on January 1st in conformity with the ancient indication of the liturgy of the city of Rome, is meant to commemorate the part played by Mary in this mystery of salvation. It is meant also to exalt the singular dignity which this mystery brings to the 'holy Mother... through whom we were found worthy to receive the Author of Life. It is likewise a fitting occasion for renewing adoration to the newborn Prince of Peace, for listening once more to the glad tidings of the angels and for imploring from God, through the Queen of Peace, the supreme gift of peace. It is for this reason that, in the happy concurrence of the Octave of Christmas and the first day of the year, we have instituted the World Day of Peace, an occasion that is gaining increasing support and already bringing forth fruits of peace in the hearts of many." *(Pope Paul VI, 'Marialis Cultus', 5)*

"Mary's Motherhood in the economy of grace has no pause in its duration from the consent that she loyally gave at the Annunciation and maintained, without faltering, at the foot of the Cross until the everlasting consummation of all the elect. Raised into heaven, she has not laid aside this saving office but persists with many pleas in winning us the gifts of divine salvation. Her motherly love makes her care for her Son's brethren still on their pilgrimage, still involved in dangers and difficulties until they shall be brought into the happiness of their Fatherland. For this reason, the Blessed Virgin is called upon in the Church under the titles of Advocate, Auxiliatrix, Adjutrix, Mediatrix." *(Lumen Gentium, 62)*

Mary is the Mother of her Son's Mystical Body, the Church, and she encourages her children to follow her example in wholehearted assent to the will of God the Father to whom she is united by the Holy Spirit. Cardinal Newman in his *'The Theory of Developments' (1843)'*, meditates on Mary's faith as much more than a passive acceptance of Divine Providence and its revelations: "Within her heart she pondered upon the visit of the shepherds who told her of the vision of angels and announced that the Infant in her arms was the Saviour who is Christ the Lord. Twelve years later, when she found her Son in the Temple and He explained how He must do the work of His Father, again she treasured these things in her heart. Her faith so anticipated His first miracle that she forewarned the servants at Cana to carry out instructions to the letter. Our Lady then, is the pattern of faith both in the reception and in the study of Divine Truth, acceptance being followed by a cherishing. Zacarias reasoned first and believed later, With love and reverence Mary believed and then reasoned."

Meaning of the feast

On this first day of a New Year as good resolutions abound, we renew our devotion to the Queen of Heaven and earth and our fidelity to those supports which the Church offers: her feasts, her Saturdays, her months of May and October, her Rosary which facilitates meditation upon the great truths of faith and our daily gratitude for the role she plays in our salvation of which her hymnology is a reminder. The ancient carol 'The Joys Seven of the Blessed Virgin' (15th Century), associates itself appropriately to this Feast as it recounts the joys she experiences:

To see Blessed Jesus Christ
when He was first her Son;
To see her own Son Jesus Christ
to make the lame to go;
to make the blind to see;
to read the Bible o'er;
to bring the dead alive;
upon the crucifix;
to see her own Son Jesus Christ
to wear the crown of Heaven.

"Father, Source of light in every age, the Virgin conceived and bore Your Son who is called Wonderful God, Prince of Peace. May her prayers, the gift of a Mother's love, be Your people's joy through all ages. May her response, born of humble heart, draw Your Spirit to rest on Your people." *(Opening Prayer of the Feast)*

"Most merciful God, enable me to receive the Body of Your only begotten Son which He took from the Virgin Mary, that I may be found worthy to be incorporated into His Mystical Body and counted among His members." *(St Thomas Aquinas, 1225-74. Preparation for Mass)*

From the readings

"When the appointed time came, God sent His Son, born of a woman, born a subject of the Law, to redeem the subjects of the Law and to enable us to be adopted as sons. The proof that you are sons is that God has sent the Spirit of His Son into our hearts: the Spirit that cries, 'Abba, Father,' and it is this that makes you a son, you are not a slave any more; and if God has made you son, then He has made you heir." *(Galatians 4:4-7)*

"The shepherds hurried away to Bethlehem and found Mary and Joseph, and the baby lying in the manger. When they saw the child they repeated what they had been told about him, and everyone who heard it was astonished at what the shepherds had to say. As for Mary, she treasured all these things and pondered them in her heart. And the shepherds went back glorifying and praising God for all they had heard and seen; it was exactly as they had been told. When the eighth day came and the child was to be circumcised, they gave him the name Jesus, the name the angel had given him before his conception." *(Luke 2:16-22)*

Some helpful reflections

"The Word took to Himself descent from Abraham, as the apostle says, and therefore it was essential that He should, in this way, be completely like His Brothers and take a body similar to ours. That is why Mary is really part of His plan, so that He may take this body from her and offer it up for us as something that is His own... The Word took this course of action so that He could take on Himself what was ours, offer it in sacrifice and do away with it altogether and then clothe us in what was His, as He inspired the apostle to say, 'This perishable nature must put on imperishability and this mortal nature must put on immortality'... the human body, from being mortal has become immortal; though being physical it has become spiritual; though made from the earth, it has passed through the gates of heaven." *(St Athanasius, d.373. Letter to Epicetus)*

"The heavens proclaim the glory of God and the firmament shows forth the work of His hands." *(Psalm 18)*

"I remember the days that are past. I ponder all Your works. I muse on what Your hand has wrought and to

You I stretch out my hands. Like a parched land my soul thirsts for You." *(Psalm 142)*

We recognise in Mary that the practice of faith and the cultivation of its habits nurtures it against inevitable human doubts. In this way it is brought to maturity and, being the subject of our earnest petition to God, finds expression in our way of living our response to God's plan for us. Through the sacred Scriptures, the liturgy and its music, the Holy Mass, Sacraments and Devotions, the Church inspires and nourishes faith in the God of the beauty and hope which surrounds us.

THE PRESENTATION OF THE LORD

February 2nd

Origins and significance

"The Feast of February 2nd (formerly The Purification or Candlemas) has been given back its ancient name, the Presentation of the Lord. It should be considered a joint commemoration of the Son and of the Mother, if we are fully to appreciate its rich content. It is the celebration of a mystery of salvation accomplished by Christ, a mystery with which the Blessed Virgin was intimately associated as the Mother of the Suffering Servant of Yahweh, as the one who performs a mission belonging to ancient Israel, and as the model for the new People of God, which is ever being tested in its faith and hope by suffering and persecution." *(Marialis Cultus 7)*

Pope John II regards this Feast in which Mary and Joseph are remembered as offering the Infant Jesus to the Lord, as an eloquent icon of the total giving of one's life, of those called to reproduce in the Church and in the world "the characteristic traits of Jesus Christ." In such a context, the Holy Father encourages us to pray for vocations to the priesthood and the religious life and to support this faithful limb of the Body of Christ. In former times the Feast was celebrated as the Purification of the Most Blessed Virgin after childbirth and Candlemas, for a candle illuminates the darkness which surrounds it and offers a sign of personal vocation to light the milieu in which one finds oneself, be it family, work, parish, Church or the wider society. Fortunately, the Holy Spirit neither waits for our perfection nor ceases to pursue our eternal well-being so there is no need to make a barrier of our inadequacies and frailty, consider our influence too trivial to matter, or be fainthearted about the consequences of commitment. St Paul encourages a trust in the power of God who has saved us and called us to be holy-not because of anything we ourselves have done but for His own kind purposes and by His own grace. *(2 Timothy 1:1-12)*

With this Feast we arrive at the end of the Christmas Festival and we carry blessed candles in procession to welcome Christ, the light of the Gentiles and the glory of His people Israel. His Presentation fulfils the law of Moses and He meets with His people.

"All powerful Father, Your Son became Man for us and was presented in the Temple. May He free our hearts from sin and bring us into Your Presence." *(Opening Prayer of the Feast)*

"Lord Jesus Christ, on this day You were presented by Your parents in the Temple, appearing among men and women in the substance of our flesh; the venerable Simeon, enlightened by the Holy Spirit, recognised You, took You in his arms and blessed You. Graciously grant that, illuminated and taught by the same Holy Spirit, we may truly acknowledge You and faithfully serve You." (*Collect for Candlemas, 12th Century*)

"Father, You revealed in Christ Your eternal plan of salvation and showed Him as a light to all peoples. Now that His glory has shone around us, You have renewed humanity in His immortal image. He shares Your eternal splendour, was presented in the Temple and was revealed by the Spirit as the glory of Israel and the light of all." (*Prefaces, Epiphany and Presentation, adapted*)

"Almighty Father, the love you offer always exceeds the furthest expression of our human longing, for You are greater than the human heart. Direct each thought, each effort of our life, so that the limits of our faults and weaknesses may not obscure the vision of Your glory or keep us from the peace You have promised." (*Prayer of the Church e.g. 3rd Sunday, Year A*)

From the readings for the feast

"The Lord God says this: Look, I am going to send my messenger to prepare a way before me. And the Lord you are seeking will suddenly enter His Temple; and the angel of the covenant whom you are longing for, yes, He is coming, says the Lord of hosts... He will purify the sons of Levi and refine them like gold and silver, and then they will make the offering to the Lord as it should be made. The offering of Judah and Jerusalem will then be welcomed by the Lord as in former days, as in the days of old." *(Malachi 3:1-4)*

"Since all the children share the same blood and flesh, Jesus too shared equally in it, so that by His death He could take away all the power of the devil, who had power over death, and set free all those who had been held in slavery all their lives by the fear of death. For it was not the angels that He took to Himself; He took to Himself descent from Abraham. It was essential that He should in this way become completely like His brothers so that He could be a compassionate and worthy high priest of God's religion, able to atone for human sins. That is, because He has Himself been through temptation He is able to help others who are tempted." *(Hebrews 2:14-18)*

"When the day came for them to be purified as laid down by the Law of Moses, the parents of Jesus took Him up to Jerusalem to present Him to the Lord - observing what stands written in the Law of the Lord: Every first born male must be consecrated to the Lord and also to offer in sacrifice, in accordance with what is said in the Law of the Lord, a pair of turtle doves or two young pigeons. Now in Jerusalem there was a man named Simeon. He was an upright and devout man; he looked forward to Israel's comforting and the Holy Spirit rested on him. It had been revealed to him by the Holy Spirit that he would not see death until he had set eyes on the Christ of the Lord. Prompted by the Spirit he came to the Temple; and when the parents brought in the child Jesus to do for Him what the law required, he took Him into his arms and blessed God; and he said: 'Now, Master, you can let your servant go in peace, just as You promised; because my eyes have seen the salvation which You have prepared for all the nations to see, a light to enlighten the pagans and the glory of Your people Israel.' He said to Mary His Mother, 'You see this Child: He is destined for the fall and for the rising of many in Israel, destined to be a sign that is rejected - and a sword will pierce your own soul too - so that the secret thoughts of many may be laid bare.' There was also a prophetess, Anna. She was now eighty-four years old and never left the Temple, serving God night and day with fasting and prayer. She... began to praise God and she spoke of the Child to all who looked forward to the deliverance of Jerusalem." *(Luke 2:22-40)*

Some helpful reflections

Simeon and Anna are central to the Gospel reading. By this world's standards neither may seem to be influential but they were chosen to welcome the Messiah and to cast light upon His future about which Mary and Joseph, like

most parents, are left wondering. The Holy Spirit inspires
them to proclaim the Saviour with joy. We join with their
welcome as, entering the house of God we recognise Him
in the breaking of bread until He comes again in glory.

The prophets had foretold the coming of the
Redeemer, God's promised Delegate upon whose arrival
the Temple would be filled with His glory and, as in the
days of old, the offerings of Judah and Jerusalem would
prove acceptable to the Lord. Our Lord's first visit to the
Temple lacked the pomp that might have been expected.
Nothing distinguished the Holy Family from other wor-
shippers as they brought their modest sacrificial offering
to satisfy the requirements of thanking God for a child
and the purification of the mother who consecrated her
infant to Him. *(cf Exodus 13:2; Leviticus 12:6-8)* The
prophecy is fulfilled and the ritual confirms that Jesus is
one with us in His humanity. The spiritual awareness of
Simeon and Anna enables them to look beyond an incon-
spicuous arrival to "the salvation prepared for all
nations". Their lifetime of prayer that the Redeemer
should come bears fruit and Simeon recognises God
made Man. Anna praises God in telling of the Child to all
who expect Jerusalem's deliverance. They represent our
own welcome and show us that the eyes of faith and a
receptive heart are more important than status in enabling
an awareness of Christ. With the young Mother we listen
to Simeon's prophecy concerning her baby Son's destiny

and the sword which was to pierce her soul, how and when she knew not. Now begins her share in the suffering and death of her Son with whom she stands to the last moment of His human life.

"Blessed is the soul which heareth the Lord speaking within her and, from the mouth, receiveth the word of consolation. Blessed are the ears that catch the pulse of the divine whisper... and... listen not after the voice which is sounding without, but for the truth teaching inwardly." Thomas a Kempis, 1380-1471, ('Of the Imitation of Christ' 3:1)

"Only faith can guarantee the blessings that we hope for, or prove the existence of the realities that at present remain unseen." *(Hebrews 11:1)*

"O Gates lift up your heads; grow higher ancient doors. Let Him enter, the King of Glory." *(Psalm 23)*

THE ANNUNCIATION OF THE LORD

March 25th

Origins and significance

Celebrated nine months before the birth of Our Lord, this is a feast of both Christ and the Blessed Virgin: "of the Word who becomes Son of Mary and of the Virgin who becomes Mother of God. With regard to Christ, the East and the West celebrate this Solemnity as the commemoration of the salvific 'fiat' of the Incarnate Word who, entering the world said: 'God, here I am! I am coming to do Your will.' They commemorate it as the beginning of the redemption and of the indissoluble and wedded union of the divine nature with human nature in the one Person of the Word. With regard to Mary, these liturgies celebrate it as a feast of the new Eve, the obedient and faithful virgin who with her generous 'fiat' became, through the working of the Spirit, the Mother of God and the true Mother of the living. By receiving into her womb the one Mediator, she became the true Ark of the Covenant and Temple of God. These liturgies celebrate it as a culminating moment in the salvific dialogue between God and man, and as a commemoration of the Blessed Virgin's free consent and co-operation in the plan of redemption." *(Pope Paul VI, 'Marialis Cultus',1974)*

By God's grace, Mary had been conceived without any stain of sin and sinless she remained throughout her life but she was subject to all the emotions and desires which we experience. The young girl was startled by the sudden arrival of an angel and his announcement of God's plan was no less disconcerting. Fear, perplexity, anticipation of society's response, and the reaction of her betrothed would have flooded her mind. Yet her faith prompted immediate consent.

We may be fearful and bewildered about God's plan for us and perhaps not recognise the value of our submission or find any comfort in it. Mary includes us in her willingness to accept with trust God's intentions so that his plan for us will be fulfilled. We are embraced in her obedience to the Divine will which marked the beginning of our salvation. The love and compassion God showed 'His servant in her lowliness' is extended to us, and Mary shares with us her magnanimity in welcoming the Saviour. She brought forth Our Lord in a unique way but we are also invited by God to bring His Son into this world by what we say and do. Mary will help us identify our personal annunciation.

"Father, You have revealed the beauty of Your power by exalting the lowly Virgin of Nazareth and making her the mother of our Saviour. Your Word became man and was born of the Virgin Mary. May we become more like Jesus Christ whom we acknowledge as our Redeemer, God and Man." *(Opening Prayer of the Feast)*

"Lord, fill our hearts with Your love and, as You revealed to us by an angel the coming of Your Son as man, so lead us through His suffering and death to the glory of His resurrection." *(Opening Prayer, 4th Sunday of Advent)*

"Father, we give thanks through Jesus Christ our Lord who came to save mankind by becoming man Himself. The Virgin Mary, receiving the angel's message in faith, conceived by the power of the Holy Spirit and bore Your Son in purest love. In Christ, the Eternal Truth, Your promise to Israel came true. In Christ, the hope of all peoples, man's hope was realised beyond all expectation." *(Preface of the Feast)*

From the readings

"The Lord Himself, therefore, will give you a sign. It is this: the maiden is with child and will soon give birth to a son whom she will call Emmanuel, a name which means God is with us." *(Isaiah 7:10-14.8:10)*

"You who wanted no sacrifice or oblation, prepared a body for me. You took no pleasure in holocausts or sacrifices for sin; then I said, just as I was commanded in the scroll of the book, 'God, here I am! I come to obey Your will". *(Hebrews 10:4-10)*

"'You are to conceive and bear a son, and You must name Him Jesus. He will be great and will be called Son of the Most High. The Lord God will give Him the throne of His ancestor David; He will rule over the house of Jacob forever and his reign will have no end.' Mary said to the angel, 'But how can this come about, for I am a virgin?', 'The Holy Spirit will come upon you,' the angel answered, and the power of the Most High will cover you with its shadow. And so the child will be holy and will be called Son of God. Know this too: your kinswoman Elizabeth has, in her old age, herself conceived a son, and she whom people called barren is now in her sixth month, for nothing is impossible to God.' 'I am the handmaid of the Lord,' said Mary, 'let what you have said be done to me.'" *(Luke 1:26-38)*

Other Reflections

"He took the form of a servant without stain of sin. He enhanced our humanity but did not thereby diminish His divinity. The emptying by which the Invisible One made Himself visible and by which the Lord and Creator of all things willed to be one with mortal men was a bending down in pity, not a failure in power... The Son of God enters the depths of this world, coming down from His heavenly throne, yet not leaving His Father's glory, begotten into a new order by a new birth." *(St Leo the Great, d.461)*

"By the mystery of this water and wine may we come to share in the Divinity of Christ who humbled Himself to share in our humanity." *(Liturgy of the Eucharist)*

"Pour forth, we beseech Thee O Lord, Thy grace into our hearts, that we, to whom the Incarnation of Christ

Thy Son was made known by the message of an angel may, by His Passion and Cross, be brought to the glory of His resurrection." *(Concluding Prayer of the 'Angelus' and Collect, March 25th, Book of Common Prayer)*

"For anyone who is in Christ there is a new creation; it was God who reconciled us to Himself through Christ and gave us the work of handing on His reconciliation... God, in Christ, was reconciling the world to Himself, not holding men's faults against them and He has entrusted to us the news that they are reconciled: So we are ambassadors for Christ; it is as though God were appearing through us, and the appeal that we make in Christ's name is: be reconciled to God. For our sake, God made the sinless One into sin, so that in Him we might become the goodness of God." *(2 Corinthians 5:17-21)*

"O Mother Blest! the chosen shrine
Wherein the Architect Divine,
Whose hand contains the earth and sky,
Vouchsafed in hidden guise to lie:
Blest in the message Gabriel brought;
Blest in the work the Spirit wrought;
Most blest, to bring to human birth
The long desired of all the earth."
(Venantius Fortunatus, c.530-600)

THE VISITATION

May 31st

Origins and significance

The liturgy of this occasion, remembered in the second Joyful Mystery of the Holy Rosary, recalls the Blessed Virgin Mary carrying her Son with her and visiting Elizabeth to offer charitable assistance and to proclaim the mercy of God the Saviour. *(Cf 'Marialis Cultus' , 7).* "Called in the Gospels 'Mother of Jesus', Mary is acclaimed by Elizabeth, at the prompting of the Holy Spirit and even before the birth of her Son, as 'the Mother of my Lord'. In fact, the One whom she conceived as man by the Holy Spirit who truly became her Son according to the flesh, was none other than the Father's eternal Son. Hence the Church confesses that Mary is truly 'Mother of God'." *(Catechism, 494-5)*

"Eternal Father, You inspired the Virgin Mary, Mother of Your Son to visit Elizabeth in her need. Keep us open to the working of Your Spirit and with Mary may we praise You for ever." *(Opening Prayer of the Feast)*

"Father, in celebrating the Visitation of the Blessed Virgin Mary, it is our special joy to echo her song of

thanksgiving. What wonders You have worked throughout the world. All generations have shared the greatness
of Your love. You looked on Mary, Your lowly servant,
and through the power of the Holy Spirit she became the
worthy Mother of Your only Son, Our Lord Jesus Christ,
who is forever the light of the world." *(Prefaces 56, 57 of
the Blessed Virgin, adapted)*

From the readings

The prophet Zephania encourages Sion, the pre-figurement
of the Church, the Bride of Christ and Mary, the Gate of
Heaven chosen to conceive the Word Incarnate. The Holy
Spirit sustains the Church till the end of time despite the
ravages wrought by human frailty. The Gates of Hell do
not prevail and Our Lord's Mother, His elected channel of
grace, consoles us that all is well: "Shout for joy, Daughter
of Sion, Israel shout aloud! Rejoice, exult with all your
heart, daughter of Jerusalem! The Lord your King is in
your midst; you have no more evil to fear... He will exult
with joy over you, he will renew you by His love."
(Zephania 3:14-18)

St Paul generates the same reassurance: "Work for the
Lord with untiring effort and with great earnestness of spirit.
If you have hope this will make you cheerful. Do not give up
if trials come and keep on praying." *(Romans 12:9-16)*

"Truly God is my salvation; I trust I shall not fear.

For the Lord is my strength, my song;

He became my Saviour.
With joy you will draw water from
the wells of salvation.

Give thanks to the Lord, give praise to His name!
Make His mighty deeds known to the peoples."
(Isaiah 12:2-6)

"When she says 'My soul magnifies the Lord and my spirit rejoices in God my Saviour', Mary acknowledges the special gifts she has been given and then the general blessings with which God never ceases to come to men's aid. 'For He who is mighty has done great things to me and holy is His name.' She attributes nothing to her own merits but speaks of the gift of the One who constantly makes His poor, weak followers into characters of great strength. So it has become an excellent practice in the Church for all to sing the Magnificat in the Office of Evening Prayer. In this way, the faithful, being reminded more often of the Incarnation, are moved to devotion and strengthened in virtue by the regular thought of the Mother's example." *(From the Homilies of St Bede the Venerable, 673-735, Bk 1:4)*

"My soul proclaims the greatness of the Lord and my spirit exults in God my Saviour; because He has looked upon His lowly handmaid. Yes, from this day forward all generations will call me blessed, for the Almighty has done great things to me. Holy is His name, and His mercy reaches from age to age for those who fear Him. He has shown the power of His arm, He has routed the proud of heart. He has pulled down princes from their thrones and exalted the lowly. The hungry He has filled with good things, the rich sent empty away. He has come to the help of Israel His servant, mindful of His mercy - according to the promise He made to our ancestors - of His mercy to Abraham and to his descendants for ever." *(Luke 1:39-56)* The Old and New Testaments enjoy a meeting in Mary's Magnificat: "May you be blessed my daughter by God most high, beyond all women on earth; and may the Lord be blessed, the Creator of heaven and earth... The trust you have shown shall not pass from the memories of men, but shall ever remind them of the power of God. God grant that you will always be held in honour and rewarded with blessings, since you did not consider your own life." *(Judith 13:18-20)*

Mary's faith was confirmed by a miracle already performed. Beyond her reasonable expectations, Elizabeth was now to give birth to Our Lord's precursor, John the Baptist. He who grants conception to the barren can also grant it to a virgin.

THE IMMACULATE HEART OF MARY

Saturday after the Second Sunday after Pentecost

Origins and significance

This Marian devotion was promoted in the seventeenth century by St John Eudes, 1601-80, who associated it with devotion to the Sacred Heart of Jesus. It flourished especially during the pontificates of Popes Pius VII and Pius XII who consecrated the world to the Immaculate Heart of Mary in 1942. This devotion to Mary is happily united in the Church's calendar to that of the Sacred Heart of her Son, the feast day of the one following that of the other.

"Let us love and honour these two hearts which are so intimately united; let us go to God the Father through the Heart of Jesus; let us go to our Saviour through the Heart of Mary. Let us render to God the Father through the Heart of Jesus what we owe to His justice and infinite bounty, and render to God the Son through the Heart of Mary what we owe to His clemency and His benefits in our regard. We shall obtain everything from the Father and the Holy Spirit through the Heart of Jesus and everything from the Son through the Heart of Mary." *(From the Manual of Prayers, Brothers of the Christian Schools, 1952.)*

Associated with this devotion is the practice of beginning each day with a prayer, the Morning Offering, by which one offers the day to God and accepts, as from the hands of God, all that comes to us in its course. The prayer relates to Our Lord's request to St Margaret Mary Alacoque and was popularised by Father Gaurelet of the Society of Jesus (1844): "O Jesus, through the Immaculate Heart of Mary, I offer You all my prayers, works and sufferings of this day, in union with the intentions of Thy Divine Heart in the Holy Mass."

"God our Father, You created a worthy dwelling place for the Holy Spirit in the Heart of the Blessed Virgin Mary. Grant that, through her prayers, we may become a fit temple for Your glory." *(Opening Prayer of the Feast)*

From the readings for the feast

"I exult for joy in the Lord, my soul rejoices in my God, for He has clothed me in the garments of salvation, He has wrapped me in the cloak of integrity, like a bridegroom wearing his wreath, like a bride adorned in her jewels." *(Isaiah 61:9-11)*

"My heart exults in the Lord, I find my strength in my God... The bows of the mighty are broken but the weak are clothed with strength; it is the Lord who gives poverty and riches. He brings men low and raises them on high. He lifts up the lowly from the dust." *(1 Samuel 2:4-8)*

"(Mary and Joseph) found Him in the Temple, sitting among the doctors, listening to them and asking them questions; and all those who heard Him were astonished at His intelligence and His replies. They were overcome when they saw Him, and His mother said to Him, 'My child, why have you done this to us? See how worried your father and I have been, looking for you! 'Why were you looking for me? He replied, 'Did you not know that I must be busy with my Father's affairs?'. But they did not understand what He meant. He then went down with them to Nazareth and lived under their authority. His mother stored up all these things in her heart." *(Luke 2:41-51)*

"As Mary pondered all she had learned from reading and from what she had heard and seen, how greatly did she increase in faith, advance in merit and become enlightened with wisdom... In everything we do, God considers our dispositions rather than our actions. And so, whether we retire mentally to God in earnest contemplation and remain at rest or whether we are intent on being of service to those around us, let our object be that we are motivated only by the love of God." *(Sermon 8, St Laurence Justinian, 1381-1455)*

THE ASSUMPTION

August 15th

Origins and significance

This glorious feast renews joy in the destiny of Mary and all who belong to the risen Christ, "the first fruits of those who have fallen asleep." *(1 Corinthians 15:20)*. Proclaiming Our Lord's victory, the seer of the Apocalypse extols His mother "adorned with the sun, the moon beneath her feet and a crown of twelve stars upon her head", a vision which embraces Sion, the faithful element of Jerusalem, the Bride, the Virgin Daughter and the Victor over the great red dragon whose machinations, throughout the ages remain thwarted. We hail Mary as the incomparable type of the Church and its most revered model. Though Queen of the Apostles and all Saints, as our Mother she remains on earth in the desert refuge prepared by God. *(cf Apocalypse 11:15-16; 12:1-17)*.

"The Immaculate Virgin, preserved from all stain of original sin, when the course of her earthly life was finished, was taken up body and soul into heavenly glory, and exalted by the Lord as Queen over all things, so that she might be the more fully conformed to her Son, the

Lord and conqueror of sin and death. The Assumption of the Blessed Virgin is a singular participation in her Son's resurrection and an anticipation of our resurrection." *(Lumen Gentium, 59)*

"The mother of Jesus, in the glory of body and soul she has attained already in heaven, is the image of the Church's attainment of glory in the age that is to come; she is the beginning of that attainment. Meanwhile, here on earth, until the day of the Lord comes, she is certainly the resplendent sign of sure hope and comfort to the pilgrim people of God.

All Christ's faithful must issue urgent pleas to the Mother of God and the Mother of men. She once assisted with her prayers at the beginnings of the Church. Now that she is placed high in heaven above all the blessed and the angels, they must plead with her to make intercession with her Son in the communion of all the saints, until the families of nations shall have the happiness of assembling in peace and harmony in a single People of God to the glory of the most Holy and Undivided Trinity." *(Lumen Gentium, 69)*

The Dogma of the Assumption

This was promulgated by Pope Pius XII in the Papal Bull *'Munificentissimus Deus'* on November 1st 1950. In the Dogma's definition, no position is taken on whether Our Lady died or not but, the faith of the Church was declared that Mary, in the fullness of her historical personality, now lives in union with the Risen Christ, her Son. The document foreshadows subsequent papal observations concerning war, the growth of materialism, the destruction of life and moral decline which can obscure our God-given identity. Mary has been given to us as the example of "the exalted destiny of both our soul and body" and the call to a growth in virtue and care for others.

"Your body, you know, is the Temple of the Holy Spirit who is in you since you received Him from God... That is why you should use your body for the glory of God." *(1 Corinthians 6:19-20)*

"All powerful and ever-living God, You raised the sinless Virgin Mary, Mother of Your Son, body and soul to the glory of heaven. May we see heaven as our final goal and come to share in her glory." *(Opening Prayer of the Feast)*

From the readings for the feast

"The woman brought forth a male child into the world, the son who was to rule all the nations with an iron scep-tre, and the child was taken up to God and to His throne, while the woman escaped into the desert, where God had made a place of safety ready. Then I heard a voice shout from heaven, 'Victory and power and empire for ever have been won by our God, and all authority for His Christ.'" *(Apocalypse 11:19; 12:1-6,10)*

"Christ has been raised from the dead, the first fruits of all who have fallen asleep. Death came through one man and, in the same way, the resurrection of the dead has come through one man. Just as all men die in Adam, so all men will be brought to life in Christ." *(1 Corinthians 15:20-26)*

"Now as soon as Elizabeth heard Mary's greeting... she... said, 'Of all women you are the most blessed, and blessed is the fruit of your womb... Yes, blessed is she who believed that the promise made her by the Lord would be fulfilled.'" *(Luke 1:39-56)*

"The reign of the Lord our God Almighty has begun; let us be glad and joyful and give praise to God because this is the time of the marriage of the Lamb. His bride is ready and she has been able to dress herself in dazzling white linen, because her linen is made of the good deeds of the saints... The dwelling of God is with men. He will dwell with them and they shall be His people and God Himself will be with them; He will wipe away every tear and death shall be no more, neither shall there be mourning nor crying nor pain any more, for the former things have passed away." *(Apocalypse 19:7-9; 21:3-4)*

"You will lament and weep but the world will rejoice. You will be sorrowful but your sorrow will be turned into joy." *(John 16:20)*

"For us, our homeland is in heaven and from heaven comes the Saviour we are waiting for... and He will transfigure these wretched bodies of ours into copies of His glorious Body." *(Philippians 3:20-21)*

Other helpful reflections

"It was fitting that she, who in giving birth had preserved her virginity unspotted, should keep her body incorrupt even after death; she who had carried the Creator as a child in her bosom should have a dwelling-place with God; the Bride espoused by the Father should dwell in the bridal chambers of heaven; she who had gazed on her Son on the Cross, receiving then in her heart the sword of sorrow she had been spared at His birth, should behold Him seated with the Father; the Mother of God should enjoy the privileges of the Son and should be honoured by all creation as the Mother and Handmaid of God."
(St John Damascene, 675-750)

"He condescended 'not to abhor the Virgin's womb'. Is it surprising then that, on the one hand, she should be immaculate in her conception or, on the other, that she should be honoured with an Assumption, and exalted as a Queen with a crown of twelve stars and the rulers of day and night to do her service? Men sometimes wonder that we call her 'Mother of life, of mercy, of salvation.' What are these titles compared to that one name, 'Mother of God'?" *(Letter to Pusey, John Henry Newman, 1864)*

OUR LADY QUEEN AND MOTHER

August 22nd

Origins and significance

After her Assumption, Mary was crowned Queen of
Heaven. This celebration of the Church's belief was instituted by Pope Pius XII in 1954, the feast day being May
31st. The liturgical Calendar now honours, on the octave
of the Assumption, the Queen who, as Mother, continues
to intercede for all her children. "On this occasion we
contemplate her who, seated beside the King of Ages,
shines forth as Queen and intercedes as Mother."
(Marialis Cultus, 7)

"She is clearly mother of the members of Christ for
she has, with love, co-operated in the birth of the faithful
in the Church, and they are the members of that head...
Mary, daughter of Adam... became the cause of salvation
for herself and for the whole human race... The Mother's
union with the Son in the work of salvation can be seen
from the time of His conception to His death". *(Lumen
Gentium, 53-59)*

"Mary and the Church are two inseparable mother-
hoods, both showing the same love which wants to

communicate itself to humanity... Assumed body and soul into the glory of Christ's Kingdom, she has become our mother in the order of grace, stays close to us on our earthly pilgrimage, supports us in our trials and shares with us the life and love of Jesus her Son." *(Catecheses, 1997, Pope John Paul II)*

"Father, You have given us the Mother of Your Son to be our Queen and Mother. With the support of her prayers may we come to share the glory of Your children in the kingdom of heaven." *(Opening Prayer of the Feast)*

From The Readings for the Feast and other Writings

"The people that walked in darkness have seen a great light; on those who live in a land of deep shadow a light has shone. You have made their gladness greater, You have made their joy increase; they rejoice in Your presence as men rejoice at harvest time, as men are happy when they are dividing the spoils... For there is a child born for us, a son given to us and dominion is laid on his shoulders... in a peace that has no end." *(Isaiah 9:1-6)*

"Mary shares our human condition but in complete openness to the grace of God. Not having known sin, she is able to have compassion on every kind of weakness. She understands sinful man and loves him with a mother's love." *(Encyclical 'Veritatis Splendor', 1993, Pope John Paul II)*

"Queen of Heaven rejoice! He whom you were found worthy to carry in your womb has risen as He said. Pray for us to God; rejoice and be glad O Virgin Mary, Alleluia. O God who gave joy to the world through the Resurrection of Your Son, we ask You that through His Mother we may obtain the happiness of eternal life."

(Regina Caeli, alternative to the Angelus at Easter time.)

THE BIRTHDAY OF THE BLESSED VIRGIN MARY

September 8th

Origins and meaning

The reading from the Book of Genesis for the feast of the
Immaculate Conception of the Most Blessed Virgin has
earlier prompted our celebration of her birthday. We have
learned of God's gracious promise of a Saviour who will
deliver us from the power of Satan. Already fashioned in
the Father's mind is Mary, the new Eve, through whom
our relationship with God, imperilled by our disobedience
in the persons of Adam and Eve, will be restored. God the
Son will become man, born not only of a woman but of a
virgin to give us second birth. His 'heel', His humanity
will be bruised by His sufferings and death as He recon-
ciles mankind with its creator.

Milton expresses the gentleness of the Father speaking
to the Son:

"O thou My sole complacence!
Well thou knowst how dear
To me are all my works, nor Man the least
Though last created, that for him I spare
Thee from my bosom and right hand, to save,

By losing thee a while, the whole race lost.
Thou therefore whom thou only canst redeem,
Their Nature to thy Nature join;
And be thyself Man among men on Earth,
Made flesh, when time shall be, of Virgin seed,
By wondrous birth..." *('Paradise Lost' Bk. 3)*

"Let us celebrate the birth of the Virgin Mary. Let us adore her Son, Christ the Lord. When the sacred virgin was born, then the world was filled with light; blessed and holy is the stock which bore such blessed fruit. With joy let us celebrate the nativity of blessed Mary so that she may intercede for us with the Lord Jesus Christ. Your birth O Virgin Mother of God, announced joy to the whole world for from you has risen the Sun of Justice. He released us from the ancient curse and made us blessed." *(The Antiphons of the Feast, Liturgy of the Hours)*

"Father of mercy, give your people help and strength from heaven. The birth of the Virgin Mary's Son was the dawn of our salvation. May this celebration of her birthday bring us closer to lasting peace." *(Opening Prayer of the Feast)*

From the readings for the feast

"You Bethlehem Ephrathah, the least of the clans of Judah, out of you will be born for me the one who is to rule over Israel; His origin goes back to the distant past, to the days of old. The Lord is therefore going to abandon them till the time when she who is to give birth gives birth... He himself will be peace." *(Micah 5:1-4)*

"We know that by turning everything to their good, God co-operates with all those who love Him, with all those that He has called according to His purpose. They are the ones He chose especially long ago and intended to become true images of His Son, so that His Son might be the eldest of many brethren. He called those He intended for this; those He called He justified, and with those He justified He shared His glory." *(Romans 8:28-30)*

"This is how Jesus Christ came to be born. His Mother Mary was betrothed to Joseph; but before they came to live together she was found to be with child through the Holy Spirit. Her husband Joseph, being a man of honour and wanting to spare her publicity. decided to divorce her informally. He had made up his mind to do this when the angel of the Lord appeared to him in a dream and said, 'Joseph, son of David, do not be afraid to take Mary home as your wife, because she has conceived what is in her by the Holy Spirit. She will give birth to a son and you must name Him Jesus because He is the one who is to save His people from their sins." *(Matthew 1:18-23)*

"So radiant, so glorious a visitation of God to men needed some prelude of joy to introduce to us the great gift of salvation... the birth of the Mother of God, and the concluding act is the union which is destined between the Word and human nature. A virgin is now born and suckled and moulded, and is made ready to be the Mother of God, the King of all forever. Let the whole creation sing praise and dance and celebrate the glories of this day. Let there be one common feast of those in heaven and those on earth. To-day, a shrine is built for the Creator of the universe. The creature is newly prepared as a divine dwelling for the Creator." *(St Andrew of Crete, 660-740)*

Joachim and Anne

As we rejoice in the birth of the Virgin Mary in her motherhood of our Saviour and of ourselves, it seems only proper to honour her own parents, St Joachim and St Anne whose feast the Church celebrates on July 26th. On our behalf they remain powerful advocates with their daughter, the Queen of Heaven. Their traditional names come to us from the *'Protovangelium of James'*, an apocryphal writing which contains an account of Our Lady's birth. The story bears a resemblance to Samuel's being born to the childless Hannah and her husband Elkanah. Devotion to St Anne dates from the sixth century although St Joachim had to wait a while longer for recognition. *(1 Samuel:1)*

Father, You gave Saints Joachim and Anne the privilege of being the parents of Mary, the Mother of Your incarnate Son. May their prayers help us to attain the salvation You have promised to Your people. *(Opening Prayer of the Feast)*

OUR LADY OF SORROWS

September 15th

Origins and significance

This title directs our minds and hearts to the spiritual
martyrdom of Our Lady in the life, passion and death of
her Divine Son and her singular participation in the work
of our salvation. By the fourteenth century Mary's
'dolours' or sorrows had been enumerated as seven: Our
Lord's circumcision, the flight into Egypt, His being lost
in Jerusalem, her meeting with Him on the road to
Calvary (the *'via dolorosa'*), His being taken down from
the Cross and His burial.

A moving and beautiful harmony emerges in the
Church's liturgical tradition which so enlivens the worship
of God. This feast follows that of the Exaltation of the Holy
Cross (now the 'Triumph of the Cross') on September 14th.
The exalted cross, the sign of our reconciliation prefigured
in Moses' raising the serpent-staff in the desert, is glorified
as the instrument of Christ's victory over death. We move
naturally to consider His Mother's contribution to that victory. Having exercised her maternal influence at the
Wedding-feast at Cana, she adopted only a supportive role

in her Son's ministry until she stands at the foot of the cross. What solace she offers us in our own grief and sufferings, temporal, futile and un-looked for though they may appear. Members of Christ's Mystical Body, with her we share in His sufferings as we anticipate the glory to come already enjoyed by this Mother of Sorrows. Pope Paul VI has described the feast as a fitting occasion for re-living "a decisive moment in the history of salvation and for venerating, together with her Son lifted up on the Cross, His suffering Mother". Christian devotion has inspired touching depictions of the Mother holding her Son's body, the most famous being Michelangelo's *'Pietà'*.

Writings and Reflections

So often, the inspiration of the liturgy, its hymns and prayers issuing from the collective wisdom and holiness of the Communion of Saints moves as we reflect.

"Holy Mother, pierce me through,
in my heart each wound renew
of my Saviour crucified.
Let me share with you His pain,
Who for all my sins was slain,
Who for me in torment died.
Can the human heart refrain
from partaking in her pain,
in that Mother's pain untold.
(From the Sequence of the Feast)

"Father, as Your Son was raised on the Cross, His Mother Mary stood by Him, sharing His sufferings. May Your Church be united with Christ in His sufferings and death and so come to share in His rising to new life." *(Opening Prayer of the Feast)*

"The martyrdom of the Virgin Mary, implicit in Simeon's prophecy, is put before us in the story of Our Lord's passion. That venerated old man, Simeon, said of the Infant Jesus: 'This Child is set for a sign that will be contradicted'; and to Mary: 'A sword will pierce your soul.' Blessed Mother, the cruel lance which opened His side and would not spare Him in death though it could do Him no injury, could not touch His soul. But it pierced your Son. His soul was no longer there but yours could not be freed and it was pierced by a sword of sorrow. We rightly speak of you as more than a martyr, for the anguish of mind you suffered exceeded all bodily pain.

'Mother behold your son.' John was given to you in place of Jesus, a disciple in place of the master, a son of Zebedee in place of the Son of God, a mere man in place of the true God. These words must have pierced your loving soul since just to recall them our hearts, hard and stony though they be." *(From the sermons of St Bernard, 1090-1153)*

"Consider the meeting of the Son and the Mother which took place on this journey (when Christ carries His Cross to Calvary). Their looks became like so many arrows, to wound those hearts which loved each other so tenderly. My sweet Jesus, by the sorrow Thou didst experience in this meeting, grant me the grace of a truly devoted love for The most holy Mother. And thou my Queen, who wast overwhelmed with sorrow, obtain for me by thy intercession, a continued and tender remembrance of the Passion of thy Son.

Consider how Our Lord had expired, was taken down from the cross by Joseph and Nicodemus who placed Him in the arms of His afflicted Mother who received Him with unutterable tenderness and pressed Him to her bosom. O Mother of Sorrow, for the love of this thy Son, accept me for thy servant and pray for me." *(4th and 13th Stations of the Cross, St Alphonsus 1696-1787).*

OUR LADY OF THE ROSARY

October 7th

Origins and significance

In October 1571, the combined forces of Spain, Venice and the Papacy defeated the Turks at the battle of Lepanto in the Mediterranean. The victors attributed their success to the patronage of the Most Blessed Virgin upon whose aid they had called by saying the Rosary. The Dominican Pope St Pius V had already been zealous in fostering devotion to the Rosary, this "compendium of the entire Gospel", and, in 1572, instituted the feast of Our Lady of the Rosary as an annual thanksgiving for the freedom of Christians from Turkish domination. October 7th became the established date for this celebration.

Four hundred years later, Pope Paul VI recalled the wonderful benefits of the practice of saying the Rosary in fostering contemplative prayer both when times are smooth and in periods of anguish and uncertainty. His words and our present Holy Father's devotion offer a timely balance when liturgical movements and renewed emphasis on reading the Scriptures might inadvertently obscure the devotion's simplicity and warmth.

"Lord, fill our hearts with Your love, and as You revealed to us by an angel the coming of Your Son as man, so lead us through His suffering and death to the glory of His Resurrection." *(Opening Prayer of the Feast)*

From the readings for the feast

"After Jesus had ascended into heaven, the Apostles went back to Jerusalem... and when they reached the city they went to the upper room where they were staying... All these joined in continuous prayer with several women including Mary, the mother of Jesus." *(Acts 1: 12-14)*

"The angel Gabriel... said to her 'Hail full of grace, the Lord is with you... You are to conceive and bear a Son and you will call Him Jesus." *(Luke 1: 26-38)*

"The Lord made me His when first He went about His work, at the birth of time, before His creation began." *(Proverbs 8: 22-24)*

"Blessed Mother and pure Virgin, renowned queen of creation, may all who keep your festival experience the power of your intercession". *(Benedictus Antiphon, Liturgy of the Hours)*

"I will greatly rejoice in the Lord, my soul shall exult in my God; for He has clothed me with the garments of salvation, He has covered me with the robe of righteousness, as a bride adorns herself with her jewels." *(cf Isaiah 61:10)*

Other Writings and Reflections

"The Word became flesh and now dwells among us, in our hearts through faith, in our memory and thoughts; he penetrates even to our imagination. For what could a man conceive of God unless he first made an image of him in his heart? He was above our understanding, unapproachable; He was completely invisible and beyond our intellect; but now He wished to be comprehended, to be seen, to be pondered.

But how? you may ask. I answer: lying in a manger, resting on a virgin's bosom, preaching on the mount, spending the night in prayer; or hanging on the cross, the pallor of death on His face, like one forsaken among the dead, overruling the powers of hell; or rising again on the third day, showing the apostles the print of the nails, the sign of victory, and finally ascending from their sight into heaven.

Is there anything that cannot be reflected on, truthfully, lovingly, reverently? If I reflect on any of these things, I reflect on God, and in all of them I find my God. I call it wisdom to meditate on these things." *(From the sermons of St Bernard,* 1091-1153)

"O God, whose only begotten Son, by His life, death and resurrection has purchased for us the rewards of eternal life, grant, we beseech You, that by meditating upon these mysteries of the most holy Rosary of the Blessed Virgin Mary, we may both imitate what they contain and obtain what they promise." *(Prayer traditionally said after saying the Rosary)*

Today's celebration inspires meditation on the mysteries of Christ, following the example of Our Lady who, in a unique way, was associated with the Incarnation, Passion and glorious Resurrection of the Son of God.

"Hail Blessed Mother full of joy
In thy consent, thy visit too:
Joy in the birth of Christ on earth,
Joy in him lost and found anew.
Hail, sorrowing in his agony-
The blows, the thorns that pierced his brow;
The heavy wood, the shameful Rood-
Yea! Queen and chief of martyrs thou.
Hail, in the triumph of thy Son,
The quickening flames of Pentecost;
Shining a Queen in light serene,
When all the world is tempest-tost."
(Augustine Rucchini, OP, 18th century)

THE PRESENTATION OF THE BLESSED VIRGIN MARY

November 21st

Origins and significance

The celebration of this feast dates back to the eighth century but earlier, in 543, November 21st had seen the dedication of the Church of Our Lady near the Temple in Jerusalem. Even in her childhood, Mary was obedient to God's will. Full of grace from the moment of her Immaculate Conception and inspired by the Holy Spirit, she consecrated herself to Him and His plan for our salvation. Today, with gratitude, we reflect upon her peerless generosity in her offering of herself in the Temple.

"Eternal Father, we honour the holiness and glory of the Virgin Mary. May her prayers bring us the fullness of Your life and love." *(Opening Prayer of the Feast)*

From the readings for the feast

"Sing, rejoice, daughter of Zion; for I am coming to dwell in your midst... The Lord will hold Judah as His portion in the Holy Land and again make Jerusalem His very own." *(Zechariah 2: 14-17)*

"Jesus was speaking to the crowds when His mother and brethren appeared; they were standing outside anxious to have a word with Him. But to the man who told Him this Jesus replied, 'Who is my mother? Who are my Brethren?' And stretching out His hand to His disciples He said, 'Here are my mother and my brethren. Anyone who does the will of my Father in heaven, he is my brother, and sister and mother." *(Matthew 12: 46-50)*

Other Reflections

"You are members of Christ's body and you are the body of Christ and this He says of you, 'Here are my mother and my brethren... We have a common heritage and Christ's heart of love would not be separated from us, though He is the only begotten. He will have us to be heirs of His Father and co-heirs with Himself. Mary by faith believed and by faith conceived, was chosen to bring forth salvation among men: by Christ created that Christ, in her, might be created, His disciple and His mother.

The Lord was journeying on and the crowds were following Him and this woman in the crowd cried out 'Blessed is the womb that bore You and the breasts You have sucked.' But they must not think blessedness lay only in bodily relationship so the Lord answered, 'Blessed rather are those who hear the word of God and keep it!... Christ the truth is in Mary's mind, Christ made flesh is in her womb." *(Sermon 25: 7-8. St Augustine, 354-430)*

THE IMMACULATE CONCEPTION

December 8th

Origins and significance

Pope Paul VI had described this feast as a "joint celebration of the Immaculate Conception of Mary, of the basic preparation for the coming of the Saviour and of the happy beginning of the Church without spot or wrinkle." Through the centuries, the Church has grown in awareness that Mary, full of grace through God, was redeemed from the first moment of her conception. *(cf Catechism of the Catholic Church, 491)*

"Eternal God, it is right that on this feast of the conception of blessed Mary, ever virgin, we should praise, bless and proclaim You with joyful hearts. By the overshadowing of the Holy Spirit she conceived Your only begotten Son and, with the glory of her maidenhood still intact, poured forth upon this world the Light Eternal, Jesus Christ our Lord." *(Pope Urban II, 1096)*

"Of long standing is that devotion of the faithful of Christ towards His most Blessed Mother, who consider that her soul, at the first instant of creation and infusion into her body was, by a special grace and privilege of

God, and in view of the merits of her Son, the Redeemer of the human race, preserved completely from the stain of original sin." *(Pope Alexander VII, December 8th 1661)*

"God, having chosen the Most Blessed Virgin from all eternity as the Mother of His Son, made her, both as to soul and body, worthy to bear Him in her womb. For this reason He preserved her from everything which might, however slightly, displease Him. Hence, by a special privilege, He exempted her from original sin. Of this we should have no doubt for it is the universal belief of the faithful and the Church sanctions it." *(St John Baptist De La Salle, 1651-1719)*

"The splendour of an entirely unique holiness by which Mary is enriched from the first moment of her conception comes wholly from Christ: she is redeemed in a more exalted fashion, by reason of the merits of her Son. The Father blessed Mary more than any other person in Christ with every spiritual blessing and chose her in Christ, before the foundations of the world, to be holy and blameless before Him in love." *(Catechism of Catholic Church, 492)*

Defined as a doctrine

In the papal bull *'Ineffabilis Deus'*, Pope Pius IX defined the doctrine of the Immaculate Conception as an article of faith on December 8th 1854. The dogma centres upon the victory of God's grace freely given in Christ. Because of sins universality, the entire human race is offered salvation through God's mercy in the life, death and resurrection of our Saviour before any merits or deserving works on our part. God's victory over sin is celebrated as Mary is conceived and her unsullied union with Him established. It will be her willing acceptance of motherhood which brings Christ to the world and our transgression, by way of our first parents is atoned. Her Son rescues from sin those already fallen and, in His Mother's case, demonstrates His redemptive power by preserving her innocence, for grace is more original than sin.

In 1947, Pope Pius XII canonised Catherine Labouré, a French Sister of Charity whose feast is December 30th. From November 27th 1830, she received visions of Our Lady who asked her to have struck the Miraculous Medal which depicts Mary standing on a globe with shafts of light coming from her hands and around her the petition 'O Mary conceived without sin, pray for us who have recourse to thee.'

"Mary Immaculate, Star of the morning,
Chosen before the creation began;
Chosen to bring for thy bridal adorning
Woe to the serpent and rescue to man."
(F.W.Wetherell, Westminster Hymnal, 1939)

Mary, conceived without sin, the first child of God, is the Mirror of Justice who reflects our present and future blessings and the truth of God's promises. Her goodness had always existed in His mind and, from eternity, He saw her 'fiat' to be freely given and that salvation was not, therefore, imposed upon His Creation. Mary's role as Mother of our Redeemer was no afterthought for with God there is the everlasting present moment, a thought which assists a vital participation in the life of the Church, her feasts and liturgical cycle which transcend historical commemoration and the limitations of vocabulary.

"Father, You prepared the Virgin Mary to be the worthy Mother of Your Son. You let her share beforehand in the salvation Christ would bring by His death and kept her sinless from the first moment of her conception. Help us by her prayers to live in Your presence without sin. She had a faith which Your Spirit prepared and a love which never knew sin. Trace in our actions the lines of her love and, in our hearts, her readiness of faith. Prepare again a world for Your Son." *(Opening Prayers of the Feast, adapted)*

"Father, You allowed no stain of Adam's sin to touch the Virgin Mary. Full of grace, she was to be a worthy Mother for Your Son, Your sign of favour to the Church at its beginning and the promise of its perfection as the Bride of Christ, radiant in beauty. Purest of virgins, she was to bring forth Your Son, the innocent Lamb who takes away our sins. You chose her from all women to be our advocate with You and our pattern of holiness." *(From the Preface of the Feast)*

From the readings for the feast

"After Adam had eaten of the tree, the Lord God called to him. 'Where are you?' He asked. 'I heard the sound of You in the garden,' he replied. 'I was afraid because I was naked, so I hid.' 'Who told you that you were naked?' He asked. 'Have you been eating of the tree I forbade you to eat?' The man replied, 'It was the woman You put with me; she gave me the fruit, and I ate it.' Then the Lord God asked the woman, 'What is this you have done?' The woman replied, 'The serpent tempted me and I ate it.' Then the Lord God said to the serpent, 'Because you have done this be accursed beyond all cattle, all wild beasts. You shall crawl on your belly and eat dust every day of your life. I will make you enemies of each other: you and the woman, your offspring and her offspring. It will crush your head and you will strike its heel.' The man named his wife 'Eve' because she was the mother of all those who live." *(Genesis 3:9-15;20)*

"The Angel Gabriel was sent by God to a town in Galilee called Nazareth, to a virgin betrothed to a man named Joseph, of the House of David; and the virgin's name was Mary. He went in and said to her, 'Rejoice, so highly favoured! The Lord is with you." *(Luke 1:26-38)*
See also the Feast of the Annunciation

THE HOLY FAMILY OF MARY AND JOSEPH

*Sunday within the octave of Christmas or December 30th
if no Sunday intervenes.*

Meaning and significance

"The shepherds hastened to Bethlehem where they found
Mary and Joseph, and the Baby lying in a manger."
(Luke 2:16; Entrance Antiphon of the Feast)

"The Church meditates with profound reverence upon
the holy life led in the house at Nazareth by Jesus, the
Son of God and Son of Man, Mary His Mother and
Joseph, the just man... There is a lesson in family life.
May Nazareth teach us what family life is, its communion
of love, its austere and simple beauty and its sacred and
inviolable character. Let us learn from Nazareth that the
formation received at home is gentle and irreplaceable.
Let us learn the importance in the social order." *(Pope
Paul VI, 'Marialis Cultus' and Homily, May 1st 1964)*

Each year, Mary and Joseph travelled to Jerusalem for
the Feast of Passover despite the rigours of the journey
and political uncertainties. They wanted to obey God's
command that the Passover be celebrated as a family and
to give good example to their Son. On the occasion with

which we are most familiar we see their fearful search for
their twelve year old, their unspeakable relief at finding
Him after three days and their parental deflation when He
explains that He must attend to His Father's affairs. We
hear the first recorded words of the Saviour and His commitment to the work of our Redemption.

Mary and Joseph guard and guide their Divine Son
who, obedient to their authority, grows to maturity
according to His unique humanity. We will mourn with
Mary in the loss of her heroic and selfless husband and
Jesus deprived of His beloved earthly guardian and men-
tor when Joseph dies, though we may envy such a death
in their presence.

Jesus, Mary and Joseph, I give you my heart
and my soul;
Jesus, Mary and Joseph, assist me in my last agony;
Jesus, Mary and Joseph, may I breathe forth my soul
in peace with You, Amen.
(Traditional Prayer)

In this Holy Family, God the Father's love has given
us an order and framework for our lives. The family, the
foundation of human society, mirrors the relationship
with God in which love and obedience leads to fulfilment
and shows to the world God's love revealed in Christ.

"Joseph dearest, Joseph mine,
Help me cradle the Child Divine;
God reward thee and all that's thine;

In Paradise. So prays the Mother Mary.
Gladly dear one, Lady mine,
Help I cradle this Child of thine;
God's own light on us both shall shine
In Paradise. So prays the Mother Mary."
(*'Song of the Crib', 15th Century*)

"Father in heaven, Creator of all, You ordered the earth to bring forth life and crowned its goodness by creating the family of man. In history's moment, when all was ready, You sent Your Son to dwell in time, obedient to the laws of life in our world. Teach us the sanctity of human love, show us the value of family life and help us to live in peace with all men that we may share in Your life forever." (*Opening Prayer of the Feast*)

"God our Father, in the Holy Family of Nazareth, You have given us the true model of the Christian home. Grant that, by following Jesus, Mary and Joseph in their love for one another and in the example of their family life, we may come to join Your home in peace and joy."
(*Evening Prayer of the Feast, Liturgy of the Hours*)

"Joseph, the Church of God protect;
Her priests with holy care endow.
Shield of the virgin-souls elect,
Hope of the fatherless be thou:
And when our parting spirits cling
To earthly joys that cannot bide,
Make Nazareth in our homes, and bring

Jesus and Mary to our side."
(R.A. Knox, 1888-1957. Westminster Hymnal 1939)

"Lord Jesus, we adore You, Son of the living God. You became Son to a human family and lived under the authority of Mary and Joseph. Teach us to walk the path of humility. Your Mother kept in her heart all that You said and did. May we learn from her example the spirit of contemplation. Help us to see our own labour as a sharing of Yours." *(Intercessions of the Feast, adapted, Liturgy of the Hours)*

From the readings for the feast

The reading from Ecclesiasticus, though predating Our Lord's birth by some two hundred years, remains relevant to contemporary family life. Parents share in God's creative act, the giving of life and the moulding of personality and His love is manifest in the tenderness they bestow when their offspring can do nothing for themselves. In their turn, children are called to be creative when the passing of time diminishes parents' powers and they realise the wonders God has wrought in the lives of their elders.

"The Lord honours the father in his children and upholds the rights of a mother over her sons. Whoever respects his father is atoning for his sins, he who honours his mother is like someone amassing a fortune. Whoever respects his father will be happy with children of his own, he shall be heard on the day when he prays, Long life comes to him who honours his father, he who sets his mother at ease is showing obedience to the Lord." *(Ecclesiasticus 3: 2-6; 12-14)*

"You are God's chosen race, His saints; he loves you and you should be clothed in sincere compassion, in kindness and humility, gentleness and patience. Bear with one another; forgive each other as soon as a quarrel begins. The Lord has forgiven you; now you must do the same... Teach each other and advise each other in all wisdom... and never say or do anything except in the name of the Lord Jesus, giving thanks to God the Father through Him." *(Colossians 3:12-21)*

"After the wise men had left, the angel of the Lord appeared to Joseph in a dream and said, 'Get up, take the child and his mother with you, and escape into Egypt, and stay there until I tell you, because Herod intends to search for the child and do away with him." So Joseph got up and, taking the child and his mother with him, left that night for Egypt, where he stayed until Herod was dead. After Herod's death, the angel of the Lord appeared in a dream to Joseph in Egypt and said, 'Get up and go back to the land of Israel, for those who wanted to kill the child are dead.' So Joseph got up and, taking the child and his mother with him, went back to the land of Israel.

COMMEMORATIONS
OF THE
MOST BLESSED VIRGIN MARY

The Roman Calendar includes commemorations related to local devotions which have acquired a wider popularity and interest. Others, originally celebrated by particular religious congregations, can be considered of significance to the whole Church by virtue of their general appeal and applicability. Happily inter-related, all contribute to acclaim the sublime place the Most Blessed Virgin occupies in Christian Worship and the example this purest of creatures gives to us.

OUR LADY OF LOURDES

February 11th

In 1858, at Lourdes in France, Our Lady appeared to Bernadette Soubirous and announced herself "I am the Immaculate Conception". She told Bernadette to bring to the attention of the world the necessity of prayer and penance. The response of the faithful has found expression in pilgrimage and the care of the sick and disabled. Lourdes remains a vibrant centre of pilgrimage and devoted faith, the scene of miraculous returns to health or peace of mind and the contented acceptance of God's will. It has been the subject of encyclicals by Popes Pius XII and John XXIII.

"God of mercy, we celebrate the feast of Mary, the sinless Mother of God. May her prayers help us to rise above our human weakness." *(Opening Prayer of the Feast)*

From the readings for the feast

"At her breast will the nurselings be carried and fondled in her lap. Like a son comforted by his mother will I comfort you". *(Isaiah 66: 10-14)*

"May you be blessed my daughter by God Most High beyond all women on earth and may the Lord be blessed, the Creator of heaven and earth... You are the glory of Jerusalem! You are the highest honour of our race." *(Judith 13: 23-24; 15: 9)*

"Blessed art thou among women and blessed is the fruit of thy womb." *(The Hail Mary, cf Luke 1: 39-56)*

"There was a wedding at Cana in Galilee. The mother of Jesus was there and His disciples had also been invited. When they ran out of wine, since the wine provided for the wedding was all finished, the mother of Jesus said to Him, 'They have no wine.' Jesus said, 'Woman, why turn to me? My hour has not come yet.' His mother said to the servants, 'Do whatever He tells you.' *(John 2: 1-11)*

OUR LADY OF FATIMA

May 13th

Background

Three young shepherds, Lucia dos Santos and her two cousins, Francisco and Jacinta Marto, declared that they had seen a vision of Our Lady at the Cova da Iria near the Portuguese town of Fatima on May 13th 1917. They described a woman in white, shedding rays of brilliant light, standing on a cloud in an evergreen tree. Having calmed their fear, the Lady asked the children to return on the thirteenth day of every month until October when she would tell them who she was and what she required of them. She requested the daily recitation of the Rosary and promised to give a sign which would quell all doubts. During subsequent visits, the children were granted apocalyptic visions and entrusted with prophetic warnings. The Lady asked that Russia be consecrated to her Immaculate Heart and that a Communion of reparation be made on the first Saturday of each month.

On October 13th 1917, the Lady identified herself as Our Lady of the Rosary and the fifty thousand people who had gathered at the Cova, despite local ridicule and scepticism, claimed to witness the 'miracle of the sun' dancing in the heavens. The children, in ecstasy, saw visions of the Holy Family, Our Lady of Sorrows and her Son and Our Lady of Mount Carmel.

Message

In 1930, the Bishop of Leiria confirmed the legitimacy of the apparitions and sanctioned the veneration of Our Lady of Fatima. During 1936-7 and 1941-2, Jacinta revealed further details of the message of Fatima: the plea for the practice of penance, the recitation of the Rosary and devotion to the Immaculate Heart of Mary. The second world war and the rise of the Soviet Union increased interest in the circumstances of Fatima and rumours of the 'third secret' revealed only to Popes, still abound.

On May 13th 1981, an assassination attempt was made on Pope John Paul II. A year later to the day, he made a pilgrimage to Fatima. In the square at the Basilica of Our Lady of Fatima, he thanked Our Lady for sparing him and, in his person, protecting the whole Church. He renewed the consecration of the world to the Immaculate Heart of Mary which had been made by his predecessor, Pope Pius XII in 1942.

Prayer

"In celebrating the memory of the Blessed Virgin Mary, it is our special joy to echo her song of thanksgiving.

What wonders You have worked throughout the world,
Father and ever-living God. All generations have shared
the greatness of Your love. When You looked on Mary
Your lowly servant, You raised her to be the mother of
Jesus Christ, Your Son, our Lord." *(From the Preface of
the Blessed Virgin Mary II)*

Our Lady Of Mount Carmel

July 16th

Background

Regarded as a sanctified place from the days of the Phoenicians, Mount Carmel was the site of the prophet Elijah's confrontation with the five hundred and fifty prophets of Baal *(1 Kings 18)*, and Isaiah had spoken of the 'majesty of Carmel' *(35:2)*. It overlooks the plains of Galilee not far from Nazareth and tradition holds that the area enjoys Our Lady's special protection. During the Crusades, Christian hermits sought refuge in the caves on its western slope and later, in the 13th century, united as the Brothers of Our lady of Mount Carmel which we now recognise as the great, mendicant religious order of the Carmelites. It is in Mary's honour that the brown scapular is worn and July 16th is her feast as Patroness of the Order.

"Father, may the prayers of the Virgin Mary protect us and help us to reach Christ her Son." *(Opening Prayer of the Feast)*

From the readings for the feast

"My soul glorifies the Lord,
My spirit rejoices in God my Saviour ...
He protects Israel His servant
remembering the mercy promised to our fathers,
to Abraham and his sons forever."
(Luke 1:46-55)

OUR LADY OF RANSOM

September 24th

Background

Sometimes called 'Our Lady of Mercy', this is the only Marian feast proper to England, reminding the country that it is the 'dowry of Mary'. In 1218, St Peter Nolasco founded a religious order, the Mercedarians, for the redemption of Christians held captive by the Moors. In the 19th century the title 'Our Lady of Ransom' was adopted by Father Philip Fletcher and Mr Lister Drummond for the Guild they founded to work for the conversion of England and the restoration of her dowry to Mary. Their intention was to achieve this through prayer to Our Lady and the English saints and martyrs, the appreciation of Catholic heritage and financial support for poor parishes.

Pope Leo XIII encouraged the devotion by establishing the Feast of September 24th for all English dioceses and was the first President of the Guild of Our Lady of Ransom.

"Lord, we have long been the dowry of Mary and subject of Peter, prince of the Apostles. Let us hold to the Catholic Faith, remain devoted to the Blessed Virgin and obedient to Peter." *(Opening Prayer of the Feast)*

"O God, Who for the deliverance of Christians from the power of the heathen, wast pleased, through the glorious mother of Thy Son to enrich the Church with a new family, we pray Thee grant that we who devotedly venerate her as the foundress of this great work, may likewise be delivered by her merits and intercession from all our sins and from bondage to the power of hell." *(Collect of the day, Missale Romanum, 1950)*

A Special Prayer

The following prayer for the conversion of England once upon a time used to follow the singing of *'O Salutaris Hostia'* at Benediction of the Most Blessed Sacrament:

"O Blessed Virgin Mary, Mother of God and our most gentle Queen and Mother, look down in mercy upon England thy 'Dowry' and upon us all who greatly hope and trust in thee.

By thee it was that Jesus, our Saviour and our Hope was given unto the world; and He has given thee to us that we might hope still more. Plead for us thy children whom thou didst receive and accept at the foot of the Cross, O sorrowful Mother.

Intercede for our separated brethren, that with us in the one true fold, they may be united to the Chief Shepherd, the Vicar of thy Son. Pray for us all dear Mother, that by faith fruitful in good works, we may all deserve to see and praise God, together with thee in our heavenly home".

Apart from its devout origin this prayer would seem to offer us an eloquent explanation of Marian Devotion and the feasts which assist its expression.

FEASTS IN THE ORDER OF MARY'S LIFE

As an alternative to chronological order of the Church's Calendar, the dates of the circumstances of Our Blessed Lady's life are listed to assist personal reflection:

Her Immaculate Conception, *December 8th*

Her Birthday, *September 8th*

Her Presentation, *November 21st*

The Annunciation, *March 25th*

Her Husband, Joseph, *March 19th*

The Visitation, *May 31st*

The Nativity of Our Lord, *December 25th*

Her Solemnity As Mother Of God, *January 1st*

The Holy Family, *Within the Octave of Christmas*

The Presentation of The Lord, *February 2nd*

Her Seven Sorrows, *September 15th*

Her Glorious Assumption, *August 15th*

Our Queen and Mother, *August 22nd*

Informative Catholic Reading

We hope that you have enjoyed reading this booklet.

If you would like to find out more about CTS booklets - we'll send you our free information pack and catalogue.

Please send us your details:

Name ....

Address ....

....

....

Postcode ....

Telephone...

Email ....

Send to: CTS, 40-46 Harleyford Road,
           Vauxhall, London
           SE11 5AY

Tel: 020 7640 0042
Fax: 020 7640 0046
Email: info@cts-online.org.uk    CTS

Acknowledgments
The CTS gratefully acknowledges use of prayers and readings from the Divine Office (Collins Publishers), reference to the Catechism of the Catholic Church (Geoffrey Chapman) and use of the Jerusalem Bible (DLT).